WITHDRAWAL

A **TRUE** BOOK™

Behind the Scenes

Animation

KARINA HAMALAINEN

Children's Press®
An Imprint of Scholastic Inc.

Content Consultant
Matthew Lammi, PhD
Assistant Professor, College of Education
North Carolina State University
Raleigh, North Carolina

Library of Congress Cataloging-in-Publication Data
Names: Hamalainen, Karina, author.
Title: Animation / by Karina Hamalainen ; content consultant: Matthew Lammi, PhD, Assistant
    Professor, College of Education, North Carolina.
Other titles: True book.
Description: New York, NY : Children's Press, an imprint of Scholastic Inc., [2017] | Series: A true
    book | Includes bibliographical references and index.
Identifiers: LCCN 2017004664 | ISBN 9780531235041 (library binding) | ISBN 9780531241479 (pbk.)
Subjects: LCSH: Animation (Cinematography)—Juvenile literature. | Animation (Cinematography)
    —History—Juvenile literature. | Animated films—Juvenile literature. | Computer animation—
    Juvenile literature.
Classification: LCC TR897.5 .H35 2017 | DDC 777.7—dc23
LC record available at https://lccn.loc.gov/2017004664

All rights reserved. Published in 2018 by Children's Press, an imprint of Scholastic Inc.
Printed in China 62

SCHOLASTIC, CHILDREN'S PRESS, A TRUE BOOK™, and associated logos are trademarks and/or
registered trademarks of Scholastic Inc., 557 Broadway, New York, NY 10012.
1 2 3 4 5 6 7 8 9 10 R 27 26 25 24 23 22 21 20 19 18

Front cover: A child imagining a large goldfish

**Back cover: Mickey Mouse
in *Steamboat Willie***

Find the Truth!

Everything you are about to read is true *except* for one of the sentences on this page.

Which one is **TRUE**?

T or F The first feature-length animated film did not make a lot of money in movie theaters.

T or F Meteorologists use animation to study and display storms.

Find the answers in this book.

3

Contents

THE **BIG** TRUTH!

Animation Is Everywhere!

Pokémon GO

A scene from
the film *Moana*

4 The Future of Animation

How will new technology improve animation?.... **31**

Warning!
Some of these projects use pointy,
sticky, hot, or otherwise risky objects.
Keep a trusted adult around to
help you out and keep you safe.

Merida in *Brave*

Finding Dory earned more money than any other animated film in 2016, making $1 billion worldwide!

CHAPTER 1

Lights, Camera, Action!

What is your favorite animated film? Was it hand-drawn? Made of clay? Or created on a computer? Animated movies are made up of multiple still images. The still images are combined to create moving images. More than 200 years ago, inventors created the first devices that could make still images move. Both live-action movies and animation were born then. As technology improves, it's becoming impossible to tell what's animated and what's real!

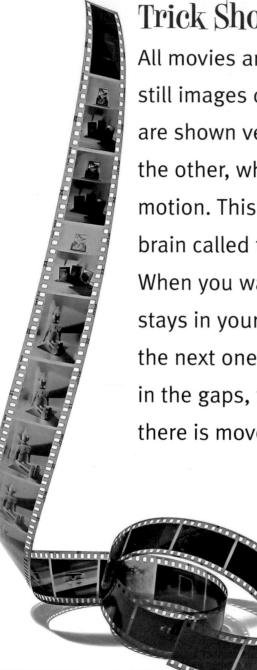

Trick Shots

All movies are made up of a series of still images called frames. The frames are shown very quickly, one right after the other, which creates the **illusion** of motion. This is due to a process in your brain called the persistence of vision. When you watch a movie, each frame stays in your mind for a split second as the next one is displayed. Your brain fills in the gaps, fooling you into thinking there is movement.

Before color film, artists sometimes added color by painting each frame by hand.

Round and Round

The first animation devices were based on circles. A British mathematician invented the zoetrope in 1834. The zoetrope is a cylinder that looks like a tiny merry-go-round on a stand. A user places strips of images inside the cylinder and then spins it. The images appear to move when the person looks through the slits in the cylinder's side. Users can change the animations by putting different image strips inside.

Eye

The faster you spin a zoetrope, the faster the images move.

Walt Disney's World

Animation continued to develop, but it didn't reach huge popularity until animators Walt Disney and Ub Iwerks released *Steamboat Willie* in 1928. This animated **short** starred a new character named Mickey Mouse. *Steamboat Willie* was the first animated film with a soundtrack that matched the action on-screen. It was a huge hit, and Disney soon became the world's most successful animator.

An Animation Timeline

1906

James Stuart Blackton creates the first animated silent film, *Humorous Phases of Funny Faces.*

1928

Steamboat Willie is released.

1937

Disney Studios releases *Snow White and the Seven Dwarfs*, the first feature-length animated film.

Movie Magic

Disney's next goal was to make a much longer, feature-length animated film. He turned to fairy tales for inspiration. *Snow White and the Seven Dwarfs* hit theaters in 1937. It raked in $8 million, making it the highest-grossing, or highest-earning, film with sound at that time. Over the next 50 years, Disney Studios released hit after hit based on fairy tales. In 1994, Disney released its first original story: *The Lion King*.

1995

Toy Story, the first computer-animated feature film, hits theaters.

2002

The Academy Awards features a category for Best Animated Film for the first time. *Shrek* wins.

2010

Toy Story 3 becomes the first animated feature to earn more than $1 billion worldwide.

An artist works on a Mickey Mouse cartoon in 1932.

Artists illustrated Disney's early films by hand. They drew characters and scenes on thousands of plastic sheets called cels. That began to change in the early 1980s. Scientists started creating computer-**generated** images for special effects in live-action movies such as *Star Wars*. In 1986, Disney partnered with a company called Pixar to make the first fully computer-animated feature film. The result was *Toy Story*. It featured **three-dimensional** (3D) characters and backgrounds. It changed animation forever.

MATH

FINDING FRAME RATES

During a movie, thousands of still images flash continuously on the screen. The number of images shown per second is called the **frame rate**. The faster the frame rate, the smoother the motion appears. Today, most movies are shot at 24 frames per second. The small cameras that athletes and adventurers often use can film at up to 240 frames per second. This helps create crisp, clear, slow-motion shots. You can use the frame rate to see how many total still images make up a movie.

Formula for finding the total number of frames:
Frame rate per second x 60 seconds per minute x movie run time in minutes

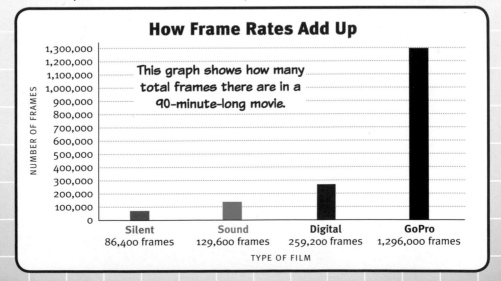

How Frame Rates Add Up

This graph shows how many total frames there are in a 90-minute-long movie.

NUMBER OF FRAMES

1,300,000
1,200,000
1,100,000
1,000,000
900,000
800,000
700,000
600,000
500,000
400,000
300,000
200,000
100,000
0

Silent	Sound	Digital	GoPro
86,400 frames	129,600 frames	259,200 frames	1,296,000 frames

TYPE OF FILM

01:13

Panel 1

PLAN
PL45/60   Durée
01:04   Panel 1

19   Panel 1

PLAN
PL52   Durée
02:12   Panel 1

PLAN
PL53   Durée
03:15   Panel 1

Panel 1

PLAN
PL55   Durée
01:23   Panel 2

PLAN
PL56   Durée
02:16   Panel 1

PLAN
Durée
02:20   Panel 1

PLAN
PL59

PLAN
PL61   Durée
01:21   Panel 1

14

CHAPTER 2

From Storyboard to Big Screen

Planning is everything when making an animated film. Before they even start animating, a creative team develops a storyboard based on the movie's script. A storyboard is like a giant comic strip that serves as the outline for the whole movie. The goal is to have a very strong idea of how every shot of the movie will look.

A storyboard for an animated feature film might include more than 25,000 images.

Artists work on the digital details of a character.

Creating Characters

Storyboard sketches are flat, or two-dimensional.
A modeler transforms the characters into 3D.
Often the first step is to make clay versions of
the characters called maquettes. Studying the
maquettes as they move helps the modelers
program the digital characters. Modelers start
with basic shapes when building characters in
a computer program. Then they add texture,
clothes, and other details. It can take two to six
months to create each character on the computer.

Setting the Scene

Other animators create the world the characters live in. Live-action movies and TV shows are filmed in real locations and on sets built in movie studios. But background artists have to create all of that from scratch for an animated film. They do everything from designing and placing the furniture in the hero's bedroom to creating a city's skyline.

Settings can be incredibly detailed works of art.

The Finishing Touches

Once most of the animation is complete, texture artists design the skin and clothes of the characters. They add details such as fabric wrinkles, bark on trees, and feathers on a bird. The more details there are, the more believable the result will be. Lighting artists program how the sun's rays or a lamp's light hit each object and create shadows. Good lighting can set a scene's mood and make a film appear more realistic.

THE PHYSICS OF FALLING

Although the animated world is created on a computer, many directors want their movies to follow real-world rules. One of the key physical rules is gravity. Animators must pay close attention to how their characters interact with it. For example, Red and his friends are launched into the sky in *The Angry Birds Movie*. They slow down as they rise in the air and then fall back toward the pig towers because of gravity.

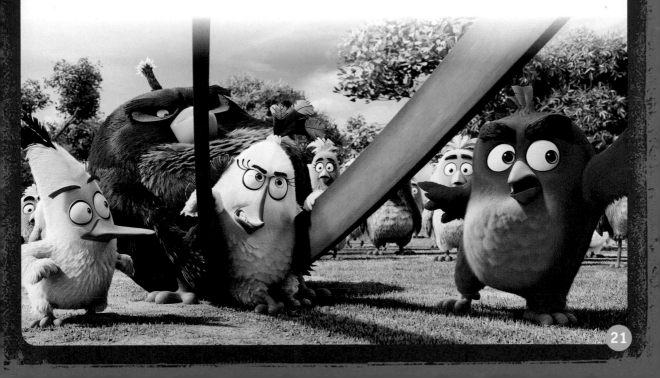

An animator uses a tablet to create sketches for a new project.

CHAPTER 3

Tools of the Trade

In the early days of animation, it was easy for small teams to create a film. But today's top animated movies are a complex blend of art and technology. It can take hundreds of people several years to complete a feature film. Each person brings an important set of skills to the team. Everyone works hard to bring the world they've dreamt up to life.

 Animators use computers that are at least four times as powerful as a home PC.

Layers of Action

Disney animators sit at tables, adding color to hand-drawn cels as camera operators shoot layered frames using a multi-pane camera.

Before computers, when animators hand-drew each frame, the background would often stay the same while the main character moved. A multi-plane camera simplified the animation process. It was a stand that held several layers of cels with a camera on top. If only the character was moving, the cel with the background image stayed put on the bottom layer. Animators only had to replace the character cel before snapping a picture of the next frame.

Clay Creations

Not every animated movie is made on computers. Stop-motion filmmakers create characters, which they place in small sets called dioramas. They set a scene and take a photo. After slightly adjusting the characters, they snap another frame. When the filmmakers use clay, like the creators of Wallace & Gromit do, it's called Claymation. Stop-motion and Claymation filmmakers need a lot of patience. It takes several days to shoot 30 seconds of Gromit wagging his tail!

Filmmakers shoot a scene for Wallace & Gromit.

25

Actor Andy Serkis performs as Gollum for *Lord of the Rings: The Two Towers.*

Animating Actors

Motion-capture technology is another way directors create lifelike, animated characters. The digital character Gollum was made this way in *The Hobbit* movies. Actor Andy Serkis wore a special jumpsuit in front of the camera. The suit had small reflective surfaces at strategic locations, such as his forearms, shins, fingers, and kneecaps. Animators used the information from the reflective dots to program the movements of the digital character.

ADDING DEPTH

Some animated films are in 3D. They require special glasses to watch them. These glasses send one image to your left eye and another image to your right eye. Slight differences in the images trick your brain into thinking that objects are jumping out of or sinking into the movie screen.

STEP 1
A pair of projectors show two slightly different images on the screen.

STEP 2
Each lens in the glasses has a different filter. This lets only one of the projected images reach each eye.

STEP 3
Because each of your eyes views things from a slightly different perspective, your brain processes the two separate images to create depth.

Animation Is

Everyone from scientists to advertisers use animation to bring their jobs to life. Read on to learn about careers outside of film studios that use animation.

Meteorologists

Advertisers

Meteorologists

Where is a hurricane going? Meteorologists collect data on wind speed, rain movements, and other factors. They enter this data into animation programs to re-create storms.

Advertisers

Graphic designers rely on animation to make the characters on your favorite cereal box move in a TV commercial.

Everywhere!

Physicists

Doctors

Physicists

Scientists at the CERN Laboratory in Switzerland are smashing together atoms, the smallest unit that a material can be broken into. They gather data to animate where the particles go after the collision!

Doctors

From monitoring the flow of blood through the body to the flow of blood in the brain, doctors use animation to check on people's health.

CHAPTER 4

The Future of Animation

Today, animation is no longer limited to the big screen. In the summer of 2016, the **augmented reality** game *Pokémon GO* took the world by storm. This game adds animated characters to your real-world surroundings on the screen of your phone. People play video games and watch shows on their phones and tablets. It's becoming more difficult to tell where real life ends and animation begins.

At its peak, more than 45 million people played *Pokémon GO* each day.

Animator Floyd Norman holds up two characters he's helped animate for Pixar Animation Studios.

Computer Power

Any new advances in animation rely heavily on advances in technology. **Rendering** is one of the most time-consuming parts of the process. It involves combining all the animation data, such as movement and texture, into sleek, detailed final images. Like each step of the stop-motion animation, computers have to painstakingly create each digital frame. Faster computers mean faster rendering, which leaves more time and money for the creative team to think up new projects.

Just Like Real Life

Animators are on a quest to make it impossible to tell the difference between the digital world and the real world. They are learning how to program the way a flock of birds moves and the way waves ripple on the ocean. Getting everything to look just right requires some studying. For example, animators working on *Moana* wanted to create realistic waves. To do so, they ran simulations of waves, just like an ocean scientist would!

Movies such as *Moana* have introduced new or more effective animation techniques.

Virtual reality immerses the user in the sights and sounds of a particular experience.

Virtual Worlds

At a 3D movie, you can look at the screen and see a ball zoom by your head. But look left or right and you see the people sitting next to you. **Immersive** technology, such as virtual reality and holograms, changes that. The animation leaps from the screen. You can fight space battles or explore strange landscapes. Turn your head and the images are all around you.

With marvels such as these already around, who knows where animation will go next? ★

VIRTUAL REALITY

The Oculus Rift is a virtual reality headset developed by Facebook. Here's a look inside it.

A screen for each eye acts much like 3D glasses.

Headphones provide sounds in sync with the images.

Face padding provides comfort.

Lenses focus light so it reaches each eye to create depth.

External tracking sensors pair with a separate tracking camera to track your head movements.

Internal tracking sensors follow your head's movements and adjust the image you see, allowing for a 360-degree view.

Make a Flipbook

A flipbook is a type of animation where a series of images are drawn on different pieces of paper. Quickly flipping through the pages creates the illusion of motion. Here's how to make your own flipbook. You can make a flipbook for any animation. For this example, we'll use a face turning from a frown into a smile.

What You Need

- ☐ scrap paper
- ☐ pencil, pen, markers
- ☐ 20 pages of sticky notes or index cards (Note: The thinner the paper is, the easier it will be to see through it and make sure your drawings are in sequence.)
- ☐ 1 small binder clip

THINK AHEAD

How are the images in a flipbook similar to the frames in an animated film?

What to Do

1. Use the scrap paper to practice drawing your faces. This will help make sure your image is consistent on each page.

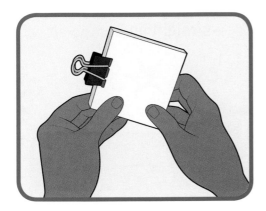

2. Stack your sticky notes or index cards neatly. Use the binder clip to secure the sticky notes on the sticky edge or the index cards on the short edge. This is your flipbook.

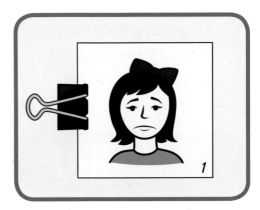

3. Number each page 1–20, in order. Draw a frowning face on page 1. This is your first **key frame**.

4. Draw a smiling face on page 20. Be sure to repeat the same exact head shape and size. If necessary, hold the pages up to a window or light and trace the shape.

5. On page 10—halfway between your beginning and end—draw a face with its mouth in a straight line.

WHAT HAPPENED?

A. What happens when you flip faster or slower?

B. How might you make the movement between the smile and frown smoother?

C. What details can you add to make the expressions more realistic?

6. On page 5, draw a face that is halfway between a frown and a flat expression. On page 15, add one that's halfway between the flat expression and the smile. Continue filling in the pages in this way.

7. When your pages are complete, hold the pages securely at the binder clip. Slowly flip the pages.

THE TRUE ANSWER

The flipbook relies on persistence of vision, just like the frames of a movie. Like any other animator, you created your cartoon frame by frame. The faster you flip through the images, the smoother the transition seems to be. You could make it even smoother by adding more frames. Details such as changes in the eyebrows, cheeks, and other features would make it more realistic.

Animate a Character

Computers interpret the motion of a character using math. You can make a shape move on a coordinate grid to map out its motion.

What You Need

- ☐ ruler
- ☐ pencil
- ☐ graph paper
- ☐ scissors
- ☐ binder clip

THINK AHEAD

How can you graph the movements of a simple, two-dimensional ball?

What to Do

1. Make the first frame. Use a ruler and pencil to draw a coordinate grid that's 10 units, or squares, long and 10 units high on your graph paper.

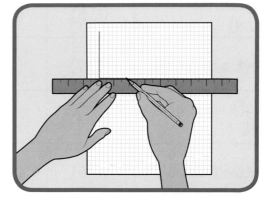

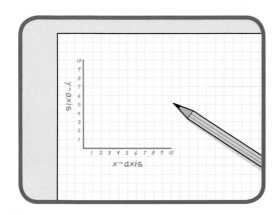

2. Label the bottom edge the x-axis, and label the left vertical edge the y-axis. Number both axes with a scale from 1 to 10.

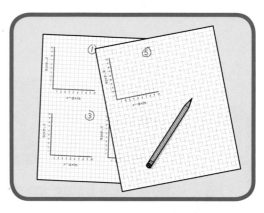

3. Repeat steps 1 and 2 until you have five separate frames. Number each frame from 1 to 5.

	Frame 1	Frame 2	Frame 3	Frame 4	Frame 5
Top of ball (x, y)	(1, 8)	(3, 5)	(5, 3)	(7, 2)	(9, 4)
Left side of ball	(0, 7)	(2, 4)	(4, 2)	(6, 1)	(8, 3)
Right side of ball	(2, 7)	(4, 4)	(6, 2)	(8, 1)	(10, 3)
Bottom of ball	(1, 6)	(3, 3)	(5, 1)	(7, 0)	(9, 2)

4. Use the chart above to draw each frame's image of a bouncing ball.

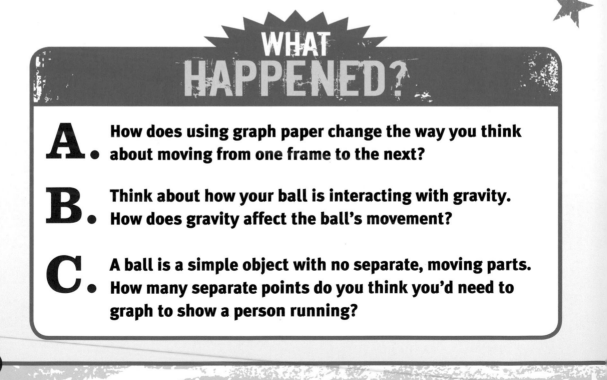

WHAT HAPPENED?

A. How does using graph paper change the way you think about moving from one frame to the next?

B. Think about how your ball is interacting with gravity. How does gravity affect the ball's movement?

C. A ball is a simple object with no separate, moving parts. How many separate points do you think you'd need to graph to show a person running?

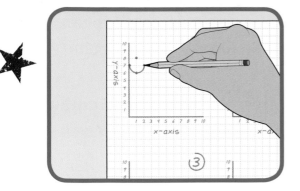

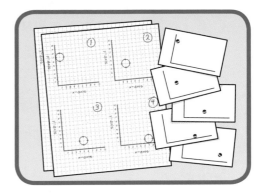

5. For each frame, plot the corresponding x and y coordinates (x, y). Use a pencil to connect the dots for each frame, rounding the edges to make a circle.

6. Cut out each frame. Stack them neatly, and secure them with a binder clip. Flip through the frames, and see your ball bounce!

THE TRUE ANSWER

This project gives you a peek at how many complicated instructions are needed to program simple movements. Even a basic two-dimensional ball has multiple points to track as it bounces. To make it realistic, animators must also account for wind, gravity, the ball's weight, and many other factors. Now imagine creating the hundreds of thousands of frames required to bounce the ball for a feature-length film!

True Statistics

First year an animated film was nominated for an Academy Award for Best Picture: 1991, for *Beauty and the Beast*

Number of artists who drew the more than 2 million planning sketches for *Snow White and the Seven Dwarfs*: 750

Number of individual pictures in the final version of *Snow White and the Seven Dwarfs*: More than 250,000

Number of Disney cartoon characters honored with a star on the Hollywood Walk of Fame as of 2018: 4 (Mickey Mouse, Snow White, Donald Duck, and Winnie the Pooh)

Amount *Frozen* made worldwide, making it the top-grossing animated film of all time as of 2018: $1,287,000,000

Did you find the truth?

F The first feature-length animated film was a financial failure.

T Meteorologists use animation to study and display storms.

Resources

Books

Hackett, Jennifer. *Game Design*. New York: Children's Press, 2018.

Labrecque, Ellen. *Multimedia Artist and Animator*. Ann Arbor, MI: Cherry Lake Publishing, 2017.

Visit this Scholastic website for more information on animation:
★ www.factsfornow.scholastic.com
Enter the keyword **Animation**

Important Words

augmented reality (AWG-men-tid ree-AL-uh-tee) technology that displays digital images and combines it with one's view of the real world

feature (FEE-chur) a full-length movie, usually 90 minutes or more

frame rate (FRAYM RAYT) the speed with which a series of images are shown in a film

generated (JEN-uh-rate-id) created or produced

illusion (i-LOO-zhuhn) something you see that does not really exist

immersive (i-MUR-siv) completely absorbing or surrounding

key frame (KEE FRAYM) a drawing that acts as a start or end point of a transition

program (PROH-gram) to give a computer or other machine instructions to make it work a certain way

rendering (REN-dur-ing) creating, as a computer program creates a frame from an animated film

short (SHORT) a film that is shorter in length than a feature film, usually running less than 40 minutes

three-dimensional (THREE duh-MEN-shuh-nuhl) having or seeming to have depth

Index

Page numbers in **bold** indicate illustrations.

About the Author

Karina Hamalainen is a writer and editor working on science and math magazines for children. She is the executive editor of *Scholastic MATH,* a magazine that connects current events to the math that students are learning in middle school. She's written stories about everything from the science of *Star Trek* to the effects of the *Deepwater Horizon* oil spill on the Gulf of Mexico. She lives in New York City.

WITHDRAWAL